Hugo's Simplified System

Dutch Verbs
Simplified

D1265252

Hugo's Language Books Ltd, London

This edition
© 1987 Hugo's Language Books Ltd
All rights reserved
ISBN 0 85285 107 3

Written by
Jane Fenoulhet M. Phil. (Dutch), M.I.L.
Lecturer in Dutch at
University College London

—

Set in 9/11pt English Times by
Printkings Ltd., Euston Road, London, NW1.
Printed and bound in Great Britain by
Anchor Brendon Ltd., Tiptree, Essex.

Contents

Introduction

The purpose of this book is to present Dutch verbs as simply and straightforwardly as possible, and to give the student all the necessary information for forming and using them. The book can be used both as a learning aid and as a reference grammar; the aim has been to avoid unnecessary detail, and the amount of information included reflects the needs of the intermediate to advanced learner. Hugo's *Dutch in Three Months* is more suitable for the complete beginner. The first part of *Dutch Verbs Simplified* deals mainly with the formation of tenses, while the second part explains their use and some other important functions of Dutch verbs.

Dutch verbs do not have complicated sets of endings: the regular verbs require only a small amount of learning and the rules have no exceptions. Even the irregular verbs do not involve a very great deal of learning. The information and rules needed for the formation of tenses will be dealt with economically to further minimize the amount of learning. Dutch verbs are not without their complexities, however, and this must be pointed out, as the student would otherwise be unprepared when encountering them, whether it be in the spoken language or in written Dutch. For example, in order to read and write Dutch verbs, the student must have mastered the *spelling rules* of Dutch. They will be given here, for your convenience. With compound tenses and compound verb constructions, it is vital to know the correct order of the different components, otherwise the meaning of the verb could be unclear. Without this additional information, the student will never be able to master Dutch verbs.

Finally, a note about the *second person* forms. Where English has only one form of the verb with 'you', Dutch has three with three different pronouns: *jij, jullie* and *u*. *Jij* and *jullie* are informal and are used to address family and friends. *Jij* is singular and *jullie* is plural. *U* is formal and is used to address strangers and superiors. It is used for both singular and plural. In recent years, the use of *jij* and *jullie* has increased so that they can now even be used with strangers. It is therefore advisable to learn <u>all</u> the 2nd person forms of the verb in Dutch. This will involve you in a small amount of extra learning.

Structure of a verb

The verb is a vital part of any language, so a thorough knowledge of verbs is essential when mastering any foreign language. Before the student can proceed to the section on Dutch verbs, he needs to be familiar with the most important terms used in describing verbs.

All the verbs in this book, be they English or Dutch, will be cited in the *infinitive* form: *hopen,* to hope; *brengen,* to bring. The infinitive is the form used in dictionary entries. It refers solely to the action denoted by the verb.

The *subject* of the verb is the doer of the action, so in

I hope   *ik hoop*
he brings   *hij brengt*

I/*ik* and he/*hij* are all subjects. A verb which can occur with just a subject is called an *intransitive* verb.

Some verbs occur with an *object* in addition to a subject. The object of a verb is the recipient of the action. In

he brings the newspaper   *hij brengt de krant*

'the newspaper' and *de krant* are both objects. A verb which occurs with an object is called a *transitive* verb.

Some verbs are used both intransitively and transitively. The example

she writes well   *zij schrijft goed*

shows the verb used intransitively and

she's writing a book   *zij schrijft een boek*

shows the verb used transitively.

The verbs in this book will usually be encountered in their *finite* form. This means they will have a subject — usually a pronoun like *ik* (I) or *zij* (she) — and an ending which is appropriate for that particular subject. We say that the verb *agrees* with the subject in *number* (singular or plural) and *person* (1st, 2nd, or 3rd).

The *tenses* of a verb are used to locate the action in time. The two main tenses are *present* and *past*. These consist of subject and finite verb. For example,

ik werk   I work   (present)
ik werkte   I worked   (past)

There are also *compound tenses* which consist of a subject, a finite *auxiliary verb* and a form of the *main* verb. For example,

hij zal komen   he will come   (future)
hij heeft gelopen   he has walked   (present perfect)

It is the auxiliary verb which agrees with the subject.

Compound verb constructions are combinations of two or more verbs. All the verbs contribute to the meaning of the overall construction: they do not merely alter the tense. For example,

zij gaat zwemmen   she is going to swim
zij wil gaan zwemmen   she wants to go and swim

Hence the need to distinguish between compound verb constructions and compound tenses.

All other terms will be explained when the relevant grammar is introduced.

Part I
How to form Dutch verbs

Auxiliary verbs

1. *Hebben* and *zijn*

Hebben (to have) and *zijn* (to be) are the most frequently used verbs in Dutch. This is because they have two different uses: first, as verbs in their own right,

Hij heeft een broer
He has a brother

Hij is aardig
He is nice

and second, as auxiliary verbs in the formation of the perfect tenses.

Hij heeft ons gezien
He has seen us

Hij is naar huis gegaan
He has gone home

For an explanation of this function, see p.24.
Hebben and *zijn* are irregular and so must be learnt.

PRESENT TENSE OF *HEBBEN*

For the student's convenience, the information given here will be as full as possible. There will be no need to repeat it every time a new verb is given. As a rule, only the most essential information will be given.

singular
1st person	*ik heb*	I have
2nd person (informal)	*jij hebt*	you have
2nd person (formal)	*u hebt/heeft*	you have
3rd person	*hij, zij, het heeft*	he, she, it has

plural		
1st person	*wij hebben*	we have
2nd person (informal)	*jullie hebben*	you have
2nd person (formal)	*u hebt/heeft*	you have
3rd person	*zij hebben*	they have

Reminder: it is necessary to learn both the 2nd person formal and informal forms.

The student will encounter both *u hebt* and *u heeft* and needs to recognize both. However, it is best to decide in advance which one you wish to use yourself and then to stick with it. Choose whichever form you find easy to remember as they are completely interchangeable.

PAST TENSE OF *HEBBEN*

singular	
had	had

plural	
hadden	had

This amount of information will suffice for the past tense of all irregular verbs as long as the student remembers that the **u-form** of the verb **is always the same as the singular** even though it is used to address one or more persons. By way of illustration, the past tense of *hebben* will be given here in full. This table can then serve as the model for all irregular verbs.

singular	
ik had	I had
jij had	you had
u had	you had
hij had	he had

plural	
wij hadden	we had
jullie hadden	you had
u had	you had
zij hadden	they had

12

PRESENT TENSE OF *ZIJN*

singular
ik ben	I am
jij bent	you are
u bent	you are
hij is	he is

plural
wij zin	we are
jullie zijn	you are
u bent	you are
zij zijn	they are

The student will encounter the form *u is,* but is advised to learn and use *u bent* which is more usual.

PAST TENSE OF *ZIJN*

singular
ik was	I was
jij was	you were
u was	you were
hij was	he was

plural
wij waren	we were
jullie waren	you were
u was	you were
zij waren	they were

2. *Zullen* and *worden*

Like *hebben* and *zijn,* these two verbs are used as auxiliary verbs. *Zullen* is used to form the future tense and the conditional of all verbs, and *worden* helps form the passive of Dutch verbs.

PRESENT TENSE OF *ZULLEN*

singular	
ik zal	I shall
jij zult/zal	you will
u zult/zal	you will
hij zal	he will

plural	
wij zullen	we shall
jullie zullen	you will
u zult/zal	you will
zij zullen	they will

All the 2nd person forms given here will be encountered.

Learning strategy: *jij zal* and *u zal* are good colloquial Dutch, so learn these for speaking. *Jij zult* and *u zult* can sound a little formal, but should certainly be learnt for writing.

PAST TENSE OF *ZULLEN*

singular	
zou	would

plural	
zouden	would

In the plural, *zouen* will also be heard. There is no need to learn this form.

PRESENT TENSE OF *WORDEN*

singular	
ik word	I become
jij wordt	you become
u wordt	you become
hij wordt	he becomes

plural

wij worden	we become
jullie worden	you become
u wordt	you become
zij worden	they become

PAST TENSE OF *WORDEN*

singular

werd	became

plural

werden	became

Worden, like *hebben* and *zijn,* is also used as a verb in its own right:

Hij wordt oud
He's getting old

Zij werd lerares
She became a teacher

Regular verbs: Formation of simple tenses

As the name implies, *regular verbs* all follow the same pattern. All you need to know is one set of basic endings for the present tense, one for the past tense, and how to form the past participle. Any new verbs in the language conform to this pattern. A knowledge of the spelling rules of Dutch is necessary. These are explained in full in *Dutch in Three Months* (Lesson One), but the most essential rules will be demonstrated below.

The verb stem

When forming the present and past tenses, the *verb stem* is always the starting-point. This is obtained by dropping the *-en* ending of the infinitive.

INFINITIVE		STEM
werken	to work	*werk*
huilen	to cry	*huil*
bouwen	to build	*bouw*

There are many verbs which are straightforward like the above examples. But there is another group which undergoes a spelling change when the *-en* ending is omitted.

INFINITIVE		STEM
haken	to hook/crochet	*haak*
hakken	to chop	*hak*
leren	to learn/teach	*leer*
leggen	to put	*leg*
horen	to hear	*hoor*
hollen	to run fast	*hol*
vuren	to fire	*vuur*
vullen	to fill	*vul*

In the above list of infinitives, *a* spells two **different** vowel sounds. The same applies to *e, o* and *u*. In each pair, e.g. *haken/hakken,* it is the second *a, e, o* or *u* which is pronounced shorter. This is reflected in the spelling, in the doubling of the next consonant, as in *hakken, leggen, hollen, vullen.* However, this device cannot be used to distinguish between the two different vowel sounds of the verb stems since there is a general spelling rule of Dutch which states that a word can never end in a doubled consonant. So *hakk* is incorrect and *hak* correct. In order now to distinguish between the two vowel sounds, e.g. in *haken* and *hakken,* once the *-en* infinitive ending has been removed, the *a, e, o,* or *u* of the infinitive is doubled for the longer vowel, giving *haak, zweer, hoor, vuur.*

The present tense

1. The basic pattern as in *werken.*

singular

ik werk	I work	= STEM
jij werkt	you work	= STEM + *t*
u werkt	you work	= STEM + *t*
hij werkt	he works	= STEM + *t*

plural

wij werken	we work	= STEM + *en*
jullie werken	you work	= STEM + *en*
u werkt	you work	= STEM + *t*
zij werken	they work	= STEM + *en*

Note that the plural forms, with the exception of *u,* are spelt in exactly the same way as the infinitive.

Above you have the basic pattern for the *present tense* of <u>all</u> Dutch regular verbs. The examples which follow are simply examples of different spelling patterns.

2. Verbs like *leren* and *leggen*.

These verbs will be shown side by side to highlight the spelling differences.

singular

ik leer	I teach	*ik leg*	I put
jij leert	you teach	*jij legt*	you put
u leert	you teach	*u legt*	you put
hij leert	he teaches	*hij legt*	he puts

plural

wij leren	we teach	*wij leggen*	we put
jullie leren	you teach	*jullie leggen*	you put _
u leert	you teach	*u legt*	you put
zij leren	they teach	*zij leggen*	they put

In the singular, the spelling consists of stem + *t,* and in the plural — as always, with the exception of *u* — the spelling is the same as that of the infinitive.

3. Verbs with a stem ending in *-t*.

Verbs like *praten* (to talk) and *zetten* (to put) do not add the *-t* ending on to the stem for the 2nd and 3rd persons singular because of the spelling rule described on p.17. Since the stem already ends in *-t,* a second *-t* cannot be added.

praten:	STEM	*praat*
zetten:	STEM	*zet*

singular

ik praat	I talk	*ik zet*	I put
jij praat	you talk	*jij zet*	you put
u praat	you talk	*u zet*	you put
hij praat	he talks	*hij zet*	he puts

plural

wij praten	we talk	*wij zetten*	we put
jullie praten	you talk	*jullie zetten*	you put
u praat	you talk	*u zet*	you put
zij praten	they talk	*zij zetten*	they put

4. Verbs with a stem ending -d.

Although -d at the end of a verb stem is actually pronounced 't', this does not affect the spelling rules which are applied in a systematic way. In the 2nd and 3rd person singular, the -t ending is therefore added as usual. For example, *branden* (to burn):

branden:	STEM	*brand*	
singular			
ik brand	I burn		STEM
jij brandt	you burn		STEM + *t*
u brandt	you burn		STEM + *t*
hij brandt	he burns		STEM + *t*

Note that -dt is pronounced 't'.

5. Verbs with f/v, s/z alternation.

Verbs which have a *v* or a *z* in the infinitive, like *geloven* (to believe) and *verhuizen* (to move house), have a stem which ends in *f* or *s* respectively.

geloven:	STEM	*geloof*
verhuizen:	STEM	*verhuis*

The present tense of such verbs is as follows:

singular
ik geloof   *ik verhuis*
I believe   I move house
jij gelooft   *jij verhuist*
you believe   you move house
u gelooft   *u verhuist*
you believe   you move house
hij gelooft   *hij verhuist*
he believes   he moves house

plural
wij geloven   *wij verhuizen*
we believe   we move house
jullie geloven   *jullie verhuizen*
you believe   you move house

u gelooft	*u verhuist*
you believe	you move house
zij geloven	*zij verhuizen*
they believe	they move house

The basic spelling rule — leaving aside the *u*-form in the plural — is:

singular: STEM ending in *-f* or *-s* + *t*
plural: as infinitive, i.e. with *-v* or *-z* + *en*.

The past tense

The starting-point for forming the *past tense* is the stem of the verb. See p.16. There are two different sets of past tense endings depending on the final letter of the stem. Verbs with stems ending in *-t, -k, -f, -s, -ch, -p* add *-te* in the singular and *-ten* in the plural (with the exception of the *u*-form). All others add *-de* in the singular and *-den* in the plural.

1. Past tense with *-t-* demonstrated using *werken* (to work).

singular		
ik werkte	I worked	STEM + *te*
jij werkte	you worked	STEM + *te*
u werkte	you worked	STEM + *te*
hij werkte	he worked	STEM + *te*
plural		
wij werkten	we worked	STEM + *ten*
jullie werkten	you worked	STEM + *ten*
u werkte	you worked	STEM + *te*
zij werkten	they worked	STEM + *ten*

There is a useful mnemonic to help you work out if a verb belongs to this group which adds *te(n)*. The Dutch word **'t kofschip** (a kind of ship) contains all the consonants which are followed by *-t-*.

2. Past tense with -d- demonstrated using *leren* (to teach/learn).

All other regular verbs, with the exception of those with *f/v, s/z* spelling alternation, form their past tense by adding *-de* to the stem in the singular and *-den* in the plural.

singular

ik leerde	I taught/learned	STEM + *de*
jij leerde	you taught/learned	STEM + *de*
u leerde	you taught/learned	STEM + *de*
hij leerde	he taught/learned	STEM + *de*

plural

wij leerden	we taught/learned	STEM + *den*
jullie leerden	you taught/learned	STEM + *den*
u leerde	you taught/learned	STEM + *de*
zij leerden	they taught/learned	STEM + *den*

3. Past tense of verbs with *f/v, s/z* spelling alternation.

Verbs like *geloven* and *verhuizen* do not obey the rules described in sections 1 and 2 for the formation of the past tense. They add *-de(n)* to the stem even though it ends in *f* and *s* respectively.

geloven (to believe):	STEM *geloof*
past tense singular:	*geloofde*
plural:	*geloofden*
verhuizen (to move house):	STEM *verhuis*
past tense singular:	*verhuisde*
plural:	*verhuisden*

21

Regular verbs:
Formation of compound tenses

The future tense

This consists of an auxiliary verb, *zullen,* which is in the present tense and agrees with the subject, followed by the *infinitive* of the main verb. The future tense of *werken* (to work) will be given in full here. In fact, it can serve as a model for <u>all</u> Dutch verbs.

singular
ik zal werken	I shall work
jij zult werken	you will work
u zult werken	you will work
hij zal werken	he will work

plural
wij zullen werken	we shall work
jullie zullen werken	you will work
u zult werken	you will work
zij zullen werken	they will work

The perfect tenses

There are three perfect tenses: *present, past* and *future.* They are formed using the simple present, past and future tenses of the auxiliary *hebben* or *zijn* + past participle of the regular verb.

1. THE PAST PARTICIPLE

The starting-point for forming the *past participle* is again the *stem* of the verb. Those verbs like *werken* with a stem ending in one of the consonants contained in *'t kofschip* add *-t* to the stem for their past participle and in addition, *ge-* is added to the front of the stem. This gives us:

	STEM	PAST PARTICIPLE
werken (to work)	*werk*	*gewerkt*
hopen (to hope)	*hoop*	*gehoopt*
wensen (to wish)	*wens*	*gewenst*

Remember that this group also formed their past tense with the addition of *-t-* to the stem.

All the other regular verbs, i.e. the ones which added *-d-* to the stem in the past tense, again add *-d* to the end of the stem, and also *ge-* to the front. This gives us:

	STEM	PAST PARTICIPLE
leren (to learn/teach)	*leer*	*geleerd*
leggen (to put)	*leg*	*gelegd*
bouwen (to build)	*bouw*	*gebouwd*

Verbs which have the following prefixes do not add *ge-*: *be-*, *er-*, *ge-*, *her-*, *ont-*, *ver-*. For example:

	PAST PARTICIPLE
behoren (to belong)	*behoord*
erkennen (to acknowledge)	*erkend*

Verbs with *f/v*, *s/z* spelling alternation are again the only exception to the above rules. Although their stems end in *f* and *s* respectively, they add *-d* to the stem to form their past participle where one would have expected *-t*. To minimize learning, simply remember that these verbs *always* add *-d* in both the past tense and past participle. Below is a list of some of the main verbs in this group:

INFINITIVE	STEM	PAST TENSE	PAST PARTICIPLE
beven to tremble	*beef*	*beefde(n)*	*gebeefd*
blozen to blush	*bloos*	*bloosde(n)*	*gebloosd*

geloven to believe	*geloof*	*geloofde(n)*	*geloofd*
grijnzen to grin	*grijns*	*grijnsde(n)*	*gegrijnsd*
leven to live	*leef*	*leefde(n)*	*geleefd*
peinzen to contemplate	*peins*	*peinsde(n)*	*gepeinsd*
reizen to travel	*reis*	*reisde(n)*	*gereisd*
streven to strive	*streef*	*streefde(n)*	*gestreefd*
verbazen to surprise	*verbaas*	*verbaasde(n)*	*verbaasd*
verdoven to anaesthetize	*verdoof*	*verdoofde(n)*	*verdoofd*

2. THE AUXILIARY VERB

There are two auxiliary verbs for forming the perfect tenses, *hebben* and *zijn*. One group of regular verbs has *hebben* as its perfect tense auxiliary, one group has *zijn,* and one group has either *hebben* or *zijn.*

a) Verbs which form their perfect tenses with *zijn.*

These are verbs which denote a change of place or state. They are always *intransitive,* i.e. used without an object. Below is a list of some common regular verbs which form their perfect tenses with *zijn:*

barsten	to burst
dalen	to descend
emigreren	to emigrate
gebeuren	to happen
groeien	to grow

immigreren	to immigrate
ontsnappen	to escape
slagen	to succeed/pass (an exam)
verouderen	to grow old
zakken	to fail (an exam)

b) Verbs which take either *hebben* or *zijn*.

These are verbs which denote some kind of locomotion. If a destination is given, they form their perfect tenses with *zijn,* otherwise, i.e. if the emphasis is on the action, rather than movement from one place to another, they take *hebben.* For example,

Ik ben naar Utrecht gefietst
I have cycled to Utrecht

The destination, Utrecht, is given, so *zijn* is used.

We hebben de hele dag gefietst
We have cycled all day long

Here, the emphasis is on the action, so *hebben* is used. Below are some examples of regular verbs which come into this category:

fietsen	to cycle
rennen	to run
roeien	to row
stappen	to step
stoppen	to stop
zeilen	to sail

c) All other verbs form their perfect tenses with *hebben*.

For example:

Wij hebben hard gewerkt
We have worked hard

Ik heb veel geleerd
I have learned a lot

3. THE PRESENT PERFECT TENSE

This tense is formed using the present tense of *hebben* or *zijn* (see section 2 above) + the past participle.

Model conjugation with *hebben* using the verb *werken* (to work):

singular
ik heb gewerkt	I have worked
jij hebt gewerkt	you have worked
u hebt/heeft gewerkt	you have worked
hij heeft gewerkt	he has worked

plural
wij hebben gewerkt	we have worked
jullie hebben gewerkt	you have worked
u hebt/heeft gewerkt	you have worked
zij hebben gewerkt	they have worked

Model conjugation with *zijn* using the verb *groeien* (to grow):

singular
ik ben gegroeid	I have grown
jij bent gegroeid	you have grown
u bent gegroeid	you have grown
hij is gegroeid	he has grown

plural
wij zijn gegroeid	we have grown
jullie zijn gegroeid	you have grown
u bent gegroeid	you have grown
zij zijn gegroeid	they have grown

4. THE PAST PERFECT TENSE

This tense is sometimes known as the *pluperfect*. It is formed using the past tense of *hebben* or *zijn* + past participle.

Model conjugation with *hebben* using the verb *geloven* (to believe):

singular

ik had geloofd	I had believed
jij had geloofd	you had believed
u had geloofd	you had believed
hij had geloofd	he had believed

plural

wij hadden geloofd	we had believed
jullie hadden geloofd	you had believed
u had geloofd	you had believed
zij hadden geloofd	they had believed

Model conjugation with *zijn,* using the verb *verhuizen* (to move house):

singular

ik was verhuisd	I had moved house
jij was verhuisd	you had moved house
u was verhuisd	you had moved house
hij was verhuisd	he had moved house

plural

wij waren verhuisd	we had moved house
jullie waren verhuisd	you had moved house
u was verhuisd	you had moved house
zij waren verhuisd	they had moved house

5. THE FUTURE PERFECT TENSE

This tense consists of 2 auxiliaries + past participle: *zullen,* the future auxiliary, is used in the present tense + the past participle + infinitive of *hebben/zijn.*

Model conjugation using the verb *werken:*

singular

ik zal gewerkt hebben	I shall have worked
jij zult/zal gewerkt hebben	you will have worked
u zult gewerkt hebben	you will have worked
hij zal gewerkt hebben	he will have worked

plural

wij zullen gewerkt hebben	we shall have worked
jullie zullen gewerkt hebben	you will have worked
u zult gewerkt hebben	you will have worked
zij zullen gewerkt hebben	they will have worked

The student will also encounter the following order of elements: *ik zal hebben gewerkt* etc. This is also perfectly acceptable. Verbs which have *zijn* as their perfect auxiliary follow the same pattern as is given in the table above:

Ik zal verhuisd zijn
I shall have moved house

Regular verbs:
The passive

All verbs encountered so far have been *active,* i.e. the subject has always been performing the action denoted by the verb. For example, in *ik geloof,* I believe, the subject is *ik* and is doing the believing. Now take the sentence

Hij maakt de foto
He takes the photo

We describe the verb as *active* because *hij,* the subject, is performing the act of taking the photo. The sentence can also be turned round to focus on the photo, with *foto* in subject position:

De foto wordt (door hem) gemaakt
The photo is taken (by him)

The above two sentences are described as *passive.*

Formation of the passive

The *passive* of Dutch verbs is formed by an auxiliary verb, either *worden* or *zijn,* + past participle. Warning: English only has one passive auxiliary, 'to be', and this can give rise to mistakes. The student is strongly advised to learn the rest of this section.

The passive of a verb has the same number of tenses as the active. *Zijn* is the passive auxiliary used in the perfect tenses, and *worden* is used for the present, past and future. For complete conjugations of both these auxiliaries, see pp.13-15.

PRESENT TENSE

This is rendered by the present tense of *worden* + past participle, as in

Het wordt gebouwd
It is (being) built

Wij worden gevolgd
We are (being) followed

PAST TENSE

This is rendered by the past tense of *worden* + past participle, as in

Zijn verhaal werd geloofd
His story was believed

De fietsen werden gemaakt
The bicycles were repaired

FUTURE TENSE

This is rendered by the present tense of *zullen* + past participle + infinitive of *worden,* as in

De auto zal gerepareerd worden
The car will be repaired

Die sonates zullen gespeeld worden
Those sonatas will be played

The order *de auto zal worden gerepareerd* is also acceptable.

PRESENT PERFECT TENSE

This consists of the present tense of *zijn* + past tense.

Ik ben gefotografeerd
I have been photographed

Die huizen zijn vorig jaar gebouwd
Those houses have been built last year

PAST PERFECT TENSE

This consists of the past tense of *zijn* + past participle, as in

De brief was naar zijn oude huis gestuurd
The letter had been sent to his old house

De mensen waren gered
The people had been rescued

FUTURE PERFECT TENSE

This tense is included here for the sake of completeness. The student is unlikely to need to use it himself. It consists of the present tense of *zullen* + past participle + infinitive of *zijn*, as in

Morgen zullen alle stemmen geteld zijn
Tomorrow all the votes will have been counted

COMPARISON OF PASSIVE FORMS IN ENGLISH AND DUTCH

The best way of eliminating errors when forming the passive in Dutch is to look at the translation of the English auxiliary verb into Dutch in the four main tenses.

the car is repaired	*de auto wordt gerepareerd*
the car was repaired	*de auto werd gerepareerd*
the car has been repaired	*de auto is gerepareerd*
the car had been repaired	*de auto was gerepareerd*

The important thing to remember is that English 'is' or 'was' is never translated by Dutch *is* or *was*.

Irregular verbs

Although it is possible to identify different categories of irregular verbs, this would only complicate matters for the student whose task is the same for all of them: they must all be learnt. **The majority of irregular verbs form their present and future tenses in the same way as regular verbs,** so only the past tense and past participle of these verbs need to be memorized.

List of irregular verbs

In this list, the following abbreviations have been used:
(h.) indicates that the verb forms its perfect tenses with *hebben*.
(z.) indicates that the verb forms its perfect tenses with *zijn*.
(h.&z.) the verb forms its perfect tenses with *hebben* or *zijn*.
* indicates irregular present tense: see following section, pp.39-41.

INFINITIVE	PAST TENSE	PAST PARTICIPLE
bakken to bake/fry	*bakte*	*(h.) gebakken*
barsten to burst	*barstte*	*(z.) gebarsten*
bederven to spoil	*bedierf*	*(h.) bedorven*
bedriegen to deceive	*bedroog*	*(h.) bedrogen*
beginnen to begin	*begon*	*(h.&z.) begonnen*
begraven to bury	*begroef*	*(h.) begraven*
begrijpen to understand	*begreep*	*(h.) begrepen*
bergen to store	*borg*	*(h.) geborgen*
besluiten to decide	*besloot*	*(h.) besloten*
bevelen to command	*beval*	*(h.) bevolen*
bewegen to move	*bewoog*	*(h.) bewogen*
bezoeken to visit	*bezocht*	*(h.) bezocht*
bezwijken to succumb	*bezweek*	*(z.) bezweken*
bidden to pray	*bad (baden)*	*(h.) gebeden*
bieden to offer	*bood*	*(h.) geboden*
bijten to bite	*beet*	*(h.) gebeten*

binden to bind	*bond*	*(h.) gebonden*
blazen to blow	*blies*	*(h.) geblazen*
blijken to turn out	*bleek*	*(z.) gebleken*
blijven to remain	*bleef*	*(z.) gebleven*
blinken to shine	*blonk*	*(h.) geblonken*
braden to roast	*braadde*	*(h.) gebraden*
breken to break	*brak (braken)*	*(h.&z.) gebroken*
brengen to bring	*bracht*	*(h.) gebracht*
buigen to bend	*boog*	*(h.&z.) gebogen*
denken to think	*dacht*	*(h.) gedacht*
doen to do	*deed*	*(h.) gedaan*
dragen to carry	*droeg*	*(h.) gedragen*
drijven to float	*dreef*	*(h.&z.) gedreven*
dringen to push	*drong*	*(h.&z.) gedrongen*
drinken to drink	*dronk*	*(h.) gedronken*
druipen to drip	*droop*	*(h.&z.) gedropen*
duiken to dive	*dook*	*(h.&z.) gedoken*
dwingen to force	*dwong*	*(h.) gedwongen*
ervaren to experience	*ervoer/ervaarde*	*(h.) ervaren*
eten to eat	*at (aten)*	*(h.) gegeten*
fluiten to whistle	*floot*	*(h.) gefloten*
gaan to go	*ging*	*(z.) gegaan*
gelden to hold good, count	*gold*	*(h.) gegolden*
genezen to cure	*genas (genazen)*	*(h.&z.) genezen*
genieten to enjoy	*genoot*	*(h.) genoten*
geven to give	*gaf (gaven)*	*(h.) gegeven*
gieten to pour	*goot*	*(h.) gegoten*
glijden to glide	*gleed*	*(h.&z.) gegleden*
glimmen to sparkle, shine	*glom*	*(h.&z.)* *geglommen*
graven to dig	*groef*	*gegraven*
grijpen to seize	*greep*	*(h.) gegrepen*
hangen to hang	*hing*	*(h.) gehangen*
hebben to have	*had*	*(h.) gehad*
heffen to lift	*hief*	*(h.) geheven*
helpen to help	*hielp*	*(h.) geholpen*
heten to be called	*heette*	*(h.)geheten*

33

hijsen to hoist	*hees*	*(h.) gehesen*
houden to hold	*hield*	*(h.) gehouden*
jagen to chase, hunt	*joeg*	*(h.) gejaagd*
kiezen to choose	*koos*	*(h.) gekozen*
kijken to look	*keek*	*(h.) gekeken*
klimmen to climb	*klom*	*(h.&z.) geklommen*
klinken to sound	*klonk*	*(h.) geklonken*
knijpen to pinch	*kneep*	*(h.) geknepen*
komen to come	*kwam (kwamen)*	*(z.) gekomen**
kopen to buy	*kocht*	*(h.) gekocht*
krijgen to get, receive	*kreeg*	*(h.) gekregen*
kruipen to creep	*kroop*	*(h.&z.) gekropen*
kunnen to be able	*kon (konden)*	*(h.) gekund**
lachen to laugh	*lachte*	*(h.) gelachen*
laden to load	*laadde*	*(h.) geladen*
laten to let	*liet*	*(h.) gelaten*
lezen to read	*las (lazen)*	*(h.) gelezen*
liegen to lie, tell lies	*loog*	*(h.) gelogen*
liggen to lie	*lag (lagen)*	*(h.) gelegen*
lijden to suffer	*leed*	*(h.) geleden*
lijken to resemble	*leek*	*(h.) geleken*
lopen to walk	*liep*	*(h.&z.) gelopen*
malen to grind	*maalde*	*(h.) gemalen*
meten to measure	*mat (maten)*	*(h.) gemeten*
moeten to have to	*moest*	*(h.) gemoeten**
mogen to be allowed	*mocht*	*(h.) gemogen**
nemen to take	*nam (namen)*	*(h.) genomen*
overlijden to die	*overleed*	*(z.) overleden*
plegen to be in the habit of	*placht*	—
prijzen to praise	*prees*	*(h.) geprezen*
raden to guess	*ried/raadde*	*(h.) geraden*
rijden to ride, drive	*reed*	*(h.&z.) gereden*
rijzen to rise	*rees*	*(z.) gerezen*
roepen to call	*riep*	*(h.) geroepen*
ruiken to smell	*rook*	*(h.) geroken*
scheiden to separate	*scheidde*	*(h.&z.) gescheiden*

schelden to scold	*schold*	*(h.) gescholden*
schenken to give, pour	*schonk*	*(h.) geschonken*
scheppen to create	*schiep*	*(h.) geschapen*
scheren to shave	*schoor*	*(h.) geschoren*
schieten to shoot	*schoot*	*(h.) geschoten*
schijnen to shine, seem	*scheen*	*(h.) geschenen*
schrijden to stride	*schreed*	*(h.&z.) geschreden*
schrijven to write	*schreef*	*(h.) geschreven*
schrikken to be frightened	*schrok*	*(h.&z.) geschrokken*
schuilen to shelter, hide	*school*	*(h.) gescholen*
schuiven to push	*schoof*	*(h.&z.) geschoven*
slaan to hit	*sloeg*	*(h.&z.) geslagen*
slapen to sleep	*sliep*	*(h.) geslapen*
slijpen to sharpen	*sleep*	*(h.) geslepen*
slijten to wear out	*sleet*	*(h.) gesleten*
sluipen to sneak, steal	*sloop*	*(z.) geslopen*
sluiten to close	*sloot*	*(h.&z.) gesloten*
smelten to melt	*smolt*	*(h.&z.) gesmolten*
smijten to throw, hurl	*smeet*	*(h.) gesmeten*
snijden to cut	*sneed*	*(h.) gesneden*
snuiven to sniff	*snoof*	*(h.) gesnoven*
spannen to stretch	*spande*	*(h.) gespannen*
spijten to be sorry	*speet*	*(h.) gespeten*
splijten to split	*spleet*	*(h.&z.) gespleten*
spreken to speak	*sprak (spraken)*	*(h.) gesproken*
springen to jump	*sprong*	*(h.&z.) gesprongen*
spuiten to spray; inject	*spoot*	*(h.&z.) gespoten*
staan to stand	*stond*	*(h.) gestaan*
steken to stab; put	*stak (staken)*	*(h.) gestoken*
stelen to steal	*stal (stalen)*	*(h.) gestolen*
sterven to die	*stierf*	*(z.) gestorven*
stijgen to rise	*steeg*	*(z.) gestegen*
stinken to stink	*stonk*	*(h.) gestonken*
stoten to push	*stiet/stootte*	*(h.&z.) gestoten*
strijden to fight	*streed*	*(h.) gestreden*
strijken to iron; stroke	*streek*	*(h.) gestreken*

stuiven to fly about; dash	*stoof*	*(h.&z.) gestoven*
treden to tread	*trad (traden)*	*(h.&z.) getreden*
treffen to hit	*trof*	*(h.) getroffen*
trekken to pull	*trok*	*(h.) getrokken*
vallen to fall	*viel*	*(z.) gevallen*
vangen to catch	*ving*	*(h.) gevangen*
varen to sail	*voer*	*(h.&z.) gevaren*
vechten to fight	*vocht*	*(h.) gevochten*
verbergen to hide	*verborg*	*(h.) verborgen*
verbieden to forbid	*verbood*	*(h.) verboden*
verdwijnen to disappear	*verdween*	*(z.) verdwenen*
vergelijken to compare	*vergeleek*	*(h.) vergeleken*
vergeten to forget	*vergat (vergaten)*	*(h.&z.) vergeten*
vergeven to forgive	*vergaf*	*(h.) vergeven*
	(vergaven)	
verlaten to leave	*verliet*	*(h.) verlaten*
verliezen to lose	*verloor*	*(h.) verloren*
vermijden to avoid	*vermeed*	*(h.) vermeden*
verraden to betray	*verried/*	*(h.) verraden*
	verraadde	
verschuilen to hide	*verschool*	*(h.) verscholen*
verstaan to understand, hear	*verstond*	*(h.) verstaan*
vertrekken to depart	*vertrok*	*(z.) vertrokken*
verzinnen to think up	*verzon*	*(h.) verzonnen*
vinden to find	*vond*	*(h.) gevonden*
vliegen to fly	*vloog*	*(h.&z.) gevlogen*
vouwen to fold	*vouwde*	*(h.) gevouwen*
vragen to ask	*vroeg*	*(h.) gevraagd*
vriezen to freeze	*vroor*	*(h.&z.) gevroren*
waaien to blow, be windy	*waaide/woei*	*(h.) gewaaid*
wassen to wash	*waste*	*(h.) gewassen*
wegen to weigh	*woog*	*(h.) gewogen*
werpen to throw	*wierp*	*(h.) geworpen*
weten to know	*wist*	*(h.) geweten*
weven to weave	*weefde*	*(h.) geweven*
wijken to give way	*week*	*(z.) geweken*
wijzen to show	*wees*	*(h.) gewezen*

willen to want	*wilde/wou (wilden)*	*(h.) gewild**
winnen to win	*won*	*(h.) gewonnen*
worden to become	*werd*	*(z.) geworden*
wreken to revenge	*wreekte*	*(h.) gewroken*
wrijven to rub	*wreef*	*(h.) gewreven*
wringen to wring	*wrong*	*(h.) gewrongen*
zeggen to say	*zei (zeiden)*	*(h.) gezegd*
zenden to send	*zond*	*(h.) gezonden*
zien to see	*zag (zagen)*	*(h.) gezien*
zijn to be	*was (waren)*	*(z.) geweest**
zingen to sing	*zong*	*(h.) gezongen*
zinken to sink	*zonk*	*(h.&z.) gezonken*
zitten to sit	*zat (zaten)*	*(h.) gezeten*
zoeken to look for	*zocht*	*(h.) gezocht*
zuigen to suck	*zoog*	*(h.) gezogen*
zuipen to booze	*zoop*	*(h.) gezopen*
zullen shall	*zou (zouden)*	*—**
zwellen to swell	*zwol*	*(h.&z.) gezwollen*
zwemmen to swim	*zwom*	*(h.) gezwommen*
zweren to swear	*zwoer*	*(h.) gezworen*
zwerven to roam	*zwierf*	*(h.) gezworven*
zwijgen to be silent	*zweeg*	*(h.) gezwegen*

Irregular verbs:
Formation of tenses

Present tense

1. Nearly all irregular verbs form their present tense in the same way as the regular verbs (see pp.17-20), so there is no new set of endings to learn. Remember that the basic spelling rules (see pp.16-17) must be applied to <u>all</u> verbs in <u>all</u> tenses. By way of illustration, the present tense of *schrijven* (to write) will be given below:

singular		
ik schrijf	I write	STEM
jij schrijft	you write	STEM + *t*
u schrijft	you write	STEM + *t*
hij schrijft	he writes	STEM + *t*

plural		
wij schrijven	we write	STEM + *en* but the *f/v*
jullie schrijven	you write	spelling rule has also been applied
u schrijft	you write	STEM + *t*
zij schrijven	they write	STEM + *en*

2. A small group of irregular verbs has an infinitive ending in -*n* rather than -*en*. These verbs form the stem by dropping the -*n* infinitive ending:

INFINITIVE	STEM
doen to do	*doe*
gaan to go	*ga*
slaan to hit	*sla*
staan to stand	*sta*
zien to see	*zie*

Note the effect of the spelling rules on the spelling of some of the vowel sounds. These verbs form their present tenses regularly, but *gaan* will be conjugated for you to show how the spelling rules operate.

singular
ik ga	I go
jij gaat	you go
u gaat	you go
hij gaat	he goes

plural
wij gaan	we go
jullie gaan	you go
u gaat	you go
zij gaan	they go

3. **komen* has an irregular present tense: the vowel sound in the singular is different from that in the infinitive and plural.

singular
ik kom	I come
jij komt	you come
u komt	you come
hij komt	he comes

plural
wij komen	we come
jullie komen	you come
u komt	you come
zij komen	they come

4. **hebben, zijn* and *zullen* all have an irregular present tense. For full conjugations, see pp. 11, 13 & 14 respectively.

5. **The other verbs with an irregular present tense are all *modal* verbs. The present tense of these verbs will be given here, but see p.64 for how to use modal verbs.

kunnen (to be able): present tense

singular
ik kan	I can
jij kunt/kan	you can
u kunt	you can
hij kan	he can

plural
wij kunnen	we can
jullie kunnen	you can
u kunt	you can
zij kunnen	they can

Both *jij*-forms are used in spoken Dutch, but *jij kunt* is used when writing Dutch. *Kunnen* has no imperative.

moeten (to have to): present tense

singular
ik moet	I must
jij moet	you must
u moet	you must
hij moet	he must

plural
wij moeten	we must
jullie moeten	you must
u moet	you must
zij moeten	they must

moeten has no imperative.

mogen (to be allowed): present tense

singular
ik mag	I may
jij mag	you may
u mag	you may
hij mag	he may

plural

wij mogen	we may
jullie mogen	you may
u mag	you may
zij mogen	they may

mogen has no imperative and no present participle.

willen (to want): present tense

singular

ik wil	I want
jij wilt/wil	you want
u wilt	you want
hij wil	he wants

plural

wij willen	we want
jullie willen	you want
u wilt	you want
zij willen	they want

Both *jij*-forms are used in spoken Dutch. The written form is *jij wilt*.

Future tense

Irregular verbs form the future tense in exactly the same way as regular
verbs (see p.22). For example:

ik zal gaan	I shall go
jij zult zien	you will see
wij zullen komen	we shall come

Past tense

Model conjugation using *helpen* (to help):

singular	
ik hielp	I helped
jij hielp	you helped
u hielp	you helped
hij hielp	he helped

plural	
wij hielpen	we helped
jullie hielpen	you helped
u hielp	you helped
zij hielpen	they helped

In the table of irregular verbs, only the past tense singular is given. For the plural, simply add *-en*. Where the plural is given between brackets, e.g. *kwam (kwamen),* this is because there is actually a change in the vowel sound from shorter *a* to longer *aa,* or because a consonant has been inserted, as in *zei (zeiden).*

Remember that **the basic spelling rules still apply when forming the plural.** For instance: *shrok, schrokken; leek, leken; schreef, schreven; prees, prezen.*

Present perfect

Once the past participle has been learnt, this tense is actually formed in exactly the same way as for regular verbs:

hebben/zijn + past participle

The rules for the selection of *hebben* or *zijn* are also the same (see pp.32-37). For example:

*Ik **heb** hem **gezien***
I have seen him

*Wij **zijn** naar huis **gegaan***
We went (lit. have gone) home

*Hij **heeft gereden***
He drove (lit. has driven)

but:

*Ik **ben** ook naar Den Haag **gereden***
I also drove (lit. have driven) to The Hague

To simplify matters, the appropriate perfect auxiliary for each irregular verb is indicated in the list on pp.32-37.

Past perfect, future perfect

Again, these tenses are formed regularly. Examples:

U had het Rijksmuseum al bezocht, nietwaar?
You had already visited the Rijksmuseum, hadn't you?

Wij waren thuis gebleven
We had stayed at home

Ik zal gegeten hebben
I shall have eaten

Jullie zullen vertrokken zijn
You will have left

The passive

Irregular verbs form the passive in exactly the same way as regular verbs, i.e. *worden* + past participle:

U wordt geroepen
You are being called

Zij werden door hun moeder gezien
They were seen by their mother

See pp.29-31 for more detail.

Part II
How to use Dutch verbs

The imperative

The imperative of the verb is used to give a command: *doe dat!* (do that!)

The imperative is formed in exactly the same way for all Dutch verbs. It consists of the stem of the verb, i.e. infinitive minus *-en*, or, in the case of the monosyllabic verbs like *doen*, infinitive minus *-n*. For example:

INFINITIVE	IMPERATIVE
werken	*werk*
bellen	*bel*
horen	*hoor*
blijven	*blijf*
lezen	*lees*
staan	*sta*

Note that the spelling rules are applied consistently.

Polite commands use the *u*-form of the verb, but reverse the order of pronoun and verb. This reverse order is known as *inversion*:

komt u hier	come here
leest u dit	read this

Questions and negations

Questions

In Dutch, the subject and verb are inverted (i.e. switched round) for questions. Note from the examples below that the English auxiliary verbs 'be' and 'do' are not translated into Dutch:

Komen zij morgen?
Are they coming tomorrow?

Neemt hij suiker?
Does he take sugar?

N.B. When the *jij*-form of the verb is inverted, the *-t* ending is dropped:

jij komt	BUT	*kom jij?*
jij blijft	BUT	*blijf jij?*
jij hoort	BUT	*hoor jij?*

Negation

Dutch verbs are negated by placing *niet* after the verb:

Zij werkt niet
She doesn't work

Wij komen niet
We aren't coming

In a sentence like 'I am not a student' or 'I haven't any children', *geen* will translate 'not a' and 'not any':

Ik ben geen student
Ik heb geen kinderen

This is explained in more detail in *Dutch in Three Months,* page 46.

Reflexive verbs

There are a number of *reflexive verbs* in Dutch. A verb is described as reflexive **when it occurs with a *reflexive pronoun* as its object,** i.e. when its subject and object are one and the same. For example:

Ik was me elke morgen
I wash (myself) every morning

In the above sentence, *ik* is the subject and *me* is the reflexive pronoun and object of the verb.

There are two kinds of reflexive verb in Dutch:

1) those which are permanently reflexive and must always occur with an object in the form of a reflexive pronoun:

Hij schaamde zich voor zijn gedrag
He was ashamed of his behaviour

Wij geneerden ons vreselijk
We were terribly embarrassed

Note that these verbs are seldom reflexive in English.

2) those which can either be reflexive or can occur as non-reflexive transitive verbs with a direct object. These are marked with an asterisk in the list on pages 52-54.

Hij scheert zich regelmatig
He shaves (himself) regularly

De kapper heeft hem gisteren geschoren
The barber shaved him yesterday

It will be clear that the first example above is of a reflexive use in which the subject and object are the same person, while the second shows a non-reflexive, transitive verb with different subject and object.

Table of reflexive pronouns

	singular	
1st person	*me*	myself
2nd person	*je*	yourself
2nd person	*u/*	yourself
formal	*zich*	yourself
3rd person	*zich*	himself

	plural	
1st person	*ons*	ourselves
2nd person	*je*	yourselves
2nd person	*u/*	yourselves
formal	*zich*	yourselves
3rd person	*zich*	themselves

Note that the 2nd person formal reflexive pronoun is either *u* or *zich*. In general, these may be used interchangeably.

Present tense (reflexive)

Model conjugation using *zich herinneren* (to remember):

singular

ik herinner me	I remember
jij herinnert je	you remember
u herinnert zich/u	you remember
hij herinnert zich	he remembers

plural

wij herinneren ons	we remember
jullie herinneren je	you remember
u herinnert zich/u	you remember
zij herinneren zich	they remember

Future tense (reflexive)

This is formed regularly with *zullen* + infinitive. The reflexive pronoun is placed immediately after the auxiliary verb with the infinitive at the end of the sentence. For example:

Zij zal zich altijd goed gedragen
She will always behave well

Past tense (reflexive)

There are both regular and irregular reflexive verbs. For example:

REGULAR: *ik ergerde me,* I was annoyed; *hij vergiste zich,* he was mistaken.

IRREGULAR: *ik sneed me,* I cut myself; *hij versliep zich,* he overslept.

Present perfect tense (reflexive)

There are both regular and irregular verbs. Once the past participles have been learnt, no extra learning is needed to form the perfect tenses of reflexive verbs. The order of elements is: *hebben/zijn* + reflexive pronoun + past participle.

Model conjugation using *zich amuseren* (to enjoy oneself):

singular
ik heb me geamuseerd	I have enjoyed myself
jij hebt je geamuseerd	you have enjoyed yourself
u hebt u geamuseerd/	you have enjoyed yourself
u heeft zich geamuseerd	you have enjoyed yourself
hij heeft zich geamuseerd	he has enjoyed himself

plural
wij hebben ons geamuseerd	we have enjoyed ourselves
jullie hebben je geamuseerd	you have enjoyed yourselves
u hebt u geamuseerd/	you have enjoyed yourselves

| *u heeft zich geamuseerd* | you have enjoyed yourselves |
| *zij hebben zich geamuseerd* | they have enjoyed themselves |

In this particular tense, the choice between *u* and *zich* as 2nd person polite reflexive pronouns is determined by the form of the auxiliary verb. If *u hebt* is selected, then *u* must be used, and *zich* must be used with *u heeft*.

Past perfect tense (reflexive)

This tense is formed in the same way as the present perfect tense except that the auxiliary verb is in the past tense. For example:

Zij hadden zich in hem vergist
They were wrong about him

Future perfect tense (reflexive)

The reflexive pronoun follows the future auxiliary and past participle + *hebben* are placed at the end of the sentence:

Zij zullen zich zeker verveeld hebben
They will certainly have been bored

List of reflexive verbs

This list gives only the most frequently used reflexive verbs. An asterisk indicates those reflexive verbs which can also be used non-reflexively with a direct object (see p.49).

*zich aankleden	to get dressed
*zich aanstellen	to show off
*zich afvragen	to wonder
*zich amuseren	to enjoy oneself
*zich bemoeien	to busy oneself

zich bevinden	to find oneself
zich bewegen	to move
zich bezighouden	to occupy oneself
zich ergeren	to get annoyed
zich gedragen	to behave
zich generen	to be embarrassed
zich haasten	to hurry
zich herinneren	to remember
zich herstellen	to recover
zich inschrijven	to enrol
zich inspannen	to exert oneself
zich melden	to report
zich noemen	to call oneself
zich omdraaien	to turn round
zich opgeven	to give oneself up
zich opstapelen	to pile up
zich opwinden	to get excited
zich schamen	to be ashamed
zich scheren	to shave
zich snijden	to cut oneself
zich terugtrekken	to withdraw
zich uitkleden	to get undressed
zich verbazen	to be amazed
zich verbeelden	to imagine
zich verbergen	to hide
zich verdedigen	to defend oneself
zich verdiepen	to immerse oneself
zich vergissen	to be mistaken
zich verheugen	to be pleased
zich verkleden	to change one's clothes
zich verlezen	to make a mistake (in reading)
zich veroorloven	to afford
zich verschrijven	to make a mistake (in writing)
zich verschuilen	to hide
zich verslapen	to oversleep
zich verslikken	to choke
zich verstoppen	to hide

*zich vervelen	to be bored
*zich voelen	to feel
*zich voorbereiden	to prepare oneself
zich voorstellen	to imagine
*zich voorstellen	to introduce oneself
*zich wassen	to wash
*zich wegen	to weigh oneself
*zich wijden aan	to devote oneself to

Separable and inseparable verbs

In Dutch it is possible to form new verbs by adding prefixes to a basic verb. For example, *gaan* can add *weg-* (away) to give *weggaan* (to go away), or *uit-* (out) to give *uitgaan* (to go out).

We shall divide verbs with prefixes into three groups: 1) those whose prefixes can never be separated from the basic verb and which are termed *inseparable;* 2) those whose prefixes are always *separable;* 3) those with prefixes which can be either *separable* or *inseparable*.

1) Inseparable

The following prefixes can never be separated from the verb:

be- as in *bemannen* (to man), *betegelen* (to tile), *behoren* (to belong). This prefix carries no stress. Verbs with unstressed prefixes form their past participle without *ge-*: *bemand, betegeld, behoord*.

de- as in *demagnetiseren* (to demagnetize); *demilitariseren* (to demilitarize). The past participle adds the *ge-* prefix to the front of the whole verb: *gedemagnetiseerd; gedemilitariseerd*.

dis- as in *dysfunctioneren* (to dysfunction); *diskwalificeren* (to disqualify). The past participle adds *ge-* to the front of the whole verb: *gedisfunctioneerd; gediskwalificeerd*.

her- as in *herontdekken* (to rediscover); *herschilderen* (to repaint); *herzien* (to revise). *Her-* is unstressed and the past participle therefore has no *ge*-prefix: *herontdekt; herschilderd; herzien*.

ont- as in *ontladen* (to unload); *ontvluchten* (to escape); *ontwaken* (to awake). Past participle: *ontladen; ontvlucht; ontwaakt*.

ver- as in *verbranden* (to burn); *verdedigen* (to defend); *vergeten* (to forget). Past participle: *verbrand; verdedigd; vergeten*.

In a sentence, prefix and verb are always written as one word:

Die mooie nieuwe auto behoort aan de buren
That lovely new car belongs to the neighbours

Hij verbrandde al zijn schoolboeken
He burned all his school books

2) Separable

The following prefixes can be separated from the verb:

aan, achter, af, bij, binnen, boven, buiten, door, heen, in, langs, mee, mis, na, neer, om, onder, op, over, rond, samen, tegen, terecht, terug, thuis, toe, uit, verder, voor, voort, weer, weg.

Separable verbs behave as follows:

Infinitive. Prefix and verb are written as one word: *aankomen* (to arrive); *inhalen* (to overtake).

Infinitive with *te*. Prefix and verb are separated by *te* and all three are written as separate words: *mee te gaan* (to go along); *op te bellen* (to ring up).

Present and past tense. Prefix and verb are separated. The prefix is placed at the end of the sentence. For example:

Hij komt morgen terug
He comes back tomorrow

Wij gingen vaak uit
We often went out

In a subclause, prefix and verb are reunited at the end of the clause:

Ik hoor dat hij morgen terugkomt
I hear that he is coming back tomorrow

Hij dacht dat wij vaak uitgingen
He thought that we often went out

Past participle. The *ge-* prefix is inserted between the separable prefix and basic verb. The suffix, i.e. *-d/-t* for regular verbs and *-en* for irregular verbs, remains the same. For example:

INFINITIVE	PAST PARTICIPLE
wegrennen to run away	*weggerend*
inpakken to wrap up	*ingepakt*
aantrekken to attract	*aangetrokken*

Imperative. Prefix and basic verb are separate. The prefix follows the imperative form of the basic verb, as in:

pas op! look out!
ga weg! go away!

The prefixes listed above on p.56 can all occur independently as prepositions and adverbs. They are used to form the largest group of separable verbs, although they are not the only kind of separable prefix. Below are some other common separable verbs with different kinds of prefixes:

ademhalen	to breathe
dichtdoen	to shut
goedkeuren	to approve
lesgeven	to teach
opendoen	to open
plaatsvinden	to take place
teleurstellen	to disappoint
vollopen	to fill up

3) Separable and inseparable

Several of the prefixes listed above in section 2) **can in fact be used inseparably as well as separably:** *aan, achter, door, mis, om, onder, over, voor, weer.* For example *ondergaan* (to go down/under) is separable, while *ondergaan* (to undergo) is inseparable.

When the verb is in the infinitive, the only difference between the separable and inseparable verb is one of stress: **all separable prefixes**

are stressed and all inseparable prefixes are unstressed. Dutch spelling sometimes uses accents to indicate stress if there is a possibility of confusion, for example:

óndergaan (separable) and *ondergáán* (inseparable)
vóórkomen to occur and *voorkómen* to prevent

In a sentence, there is less likelihood of confusion because separable and inseparable verbs behave differently.

PRESENT TENSE
Het komt vaak voor   separable
It often happens
Je voorkomt het makkelijk   inseparable
You (can) easily prevent it

PAST TENSE
De zon ging onder   separable
The sun went down
Hij onderging een zware operatie   inseparable
He underwent a serious operation

PERFECT TENSE
De boodschap is goed overgekomen   separable
The message has come across well
Zoiets is mij nog nooit overkomen   inseparable
Nothing like that has ever happened to
    me

Another difference between separable and inseparable verbs is that usually, the meaning of the separable verb is closer to the meaning of the separate parts, e.g. *óver* + *komen* = come over/across; *ónder* + *gaan* = go under/down, whereas *overkómen* (to happen) and *ondergáán* (to undergo) have acquired a special meaning.

Impersonal verbs

Impersonal verbs have *het* (it) as their subject, for example: *het regent* (it is raining).

The verbs in the following list are always impersonal, both in Dutch and in English:

bliksemen	*het bliksemt*	it is lightning
dauwen	*het dauwt*	there is a dew
donderen	*het dondert*	it is thundering
dooien	*het dooit*	it is thawing
hagelen	*het hagelt*	it is hailing
ijzelen	*het ijzelt*	it is freezing over
miezeren	*het miezert*	it is drizzling
misten	*het mist*	it is misty
onweren	*het onweert*	there is a thunderstorm
regenen	*het regent*	it is raining
sneeuwen	*het sneeuwt*	it is snowing
vriezen	*het vriest*	it is freezing

The above verbs all describe weather conditions. There are two other frequently used impersonal verbs, *lukken* and *spijten,* which are personal in English:

lukken	*het is me gelukt*	I succeeded
spijten	*het spijt me*	I am sorry

There is another group of verbs which can be used both with an impersonal subject and with a personal subject. Some common ones are:

*bevallen**	*het bevalt me*	I like it
	hij bevalt me	he pleases me/I like him
meevallen	*het valt mee*	it's better than expected
	hij viel me mee	he surprised me
spoken	*het spookt hier*	it's haunted here
	zij spookt door het huis	she prowls through the house

59

tegenvallen	*het viel tegen*	it didn't live up to expectations
	hij viel me tegen	he didn't live up to expectations
tochten	*het tocht hier*	it is draughty here
	dat raam tocht erg	that window is very draughty
verbazen*	*het verbaast me*	I'm amazed
	ik verbaas me	I am amazed
verheugen*	*het verheugt me*	I'm pleased
	ik verheug me erop	I'm looking forward to it
verwonderen*	*het verwondert me*	I'm surprised
	zijn optreden ver-wondert me	his behaviour surprises me
waaien	*het waait*	it is windy
	de wind waait	the wind is blowing

* These verbs are impersonal in Dutch, but are usually personal in English.

Impersonal constructions

All impersonal verbs employ the construction *het* + **impersonal verb.** Here the subject of the verb, *het,* does not indicate any person or thing. As in *het regent,* it serves to place the emphasis on the verb.

Another impersonal construction in Dutch is *men* + **verb.** It is used to convey that the action denoted by the verb is being performed, but by an unknown subject. Like the construction *het* + verb, it can be translated by 'it is ...' or by 'one ...'. For example:

men zegt	it is said
men vindt	one finds

This construction is also used to avoid a passive:

Men spreekt hier Nederlands
Dutch is spoken here

There is an impersonal construction which uses a passive verb: **er** +
passive verb.

Er wordt vandaag gewassen
It is washday today (*lit.* 'there is washing being done today')

Er werd gelachen
There was laughing/laughter

The present participle and its uses

The present participle is formed by adding *-d(e)* to the infinitive: *zijnde* (being); *huilend* (crying); *lachend* (laughing); *schrijvend* (writing); *wandelend* (walking). The *-d* ending is more usual, although *-de* is also found, especially in fixed expressions. For example:

Al doende leert men
Practice makes perfect

Although English does have a present participle, as in 'walk*ing*', its use differs from that of the present participle in Dutch. The construction using the verb 'to be' + present participle ('Mary is crying') is not rendered by a present participle in Dutch but by **the present tense of the verb,** in this case *huilen: Mary huilt.* See also pp.82-83.

As in English, the Dutch present participle can be used as an adjective. This means that it is subject to the normal rules for inflection of adjectives, i.e. it must add *-e* under certain circumstances. (The rules are given in *Dutch in Three Months,* p.82.) For example:

een wandelend woordenboek   a walking dictionary
een bloeiende appelboom   a blossoming apple tree
het komende jaar   the coming year
volgende week   next week

The present participle in Dutch can also be used as an adverb:

Ze kwam lachend de kamer binnen
She came into the room laughing

Hij liep grommend weg
He walked away grumbling

Uses of the infinitive

The infinitive can be used in Dutch to give commands:

Niet doen!	Don't do it!
Niet roken	No smoking!
Weggaan!	Go away!
Afblijven!	Keep off!

The infinitive can also be used as a noun which denotes the action of the verb. This noun is always neuter, i.e. it is preceded by *het*. For example:

Het roken
Smoking

Het leren van vreemde talen
The learning of foreign languages

Compound verbal constructions: Modal verbs, and others

Dutch has many phrases consisting of two or more verbs where it is necessary to know their correct order and form. Such compound verbal constructions may include *modal* verbs, *positional* verbs, or others used in a particular way. First, we shall discuss the modals.

A verb is described as modal when it expresses the speaker's attitude to what is being said in the rest of the sentence. For example, in

It **must** be an excellent film
Het moet een uitstekende film zijn

the modal verb (**must**/*moet*) tells us that the speaker is fairly sure the film is good, whereas in the following sentence

It **might** be an excellent film
Het kan een uitstekende film zijn

the modal verb (**might**/*kan*) tells us that the speaker is in considerably more doubt about the quality of the film.

Below are listed two groups of modal verbs. The verbs in group 1 are used in conjunction with an infinitive which is placed at the end of the sentence. The verbs in group 2 are used with an infinitive preceded by *te* which is placed at the end of the sentence.

1) *kunnen, moeten, mogen, willen, zullen;* how to use them

The verbs in this group are not exclusively modal auxiliaries: their other uses will also be given below.

I   *kunnen* expresses possibility when used modally. *Kunnen* itself can only occur in the present and past tenses in this function.

   *Dat **kan** wel het geval zijn*
   That might well be the case

Here the verbal construction consists of modal in 2nd place + infinitive in final position.

The other verb *can* occur as a perfect:

   *Jan **kan** al aangekomen zijn*
   Jan might have already arrived

Here the verb phrase consists of modal in 2nd place + (past participle + infinitive of perfect auxiliary). The last two verbal elements cannot be split up and are placed in final position.

In a subclause (see *Dutch in Three Months,* p.119), all the verbal elements are grouped at the end of the clause, the most usual order being past participle + modal + infinitive perfect auxiliary:

   *Ik vermoed dat Jan al aangekomen **kan** zijn*
   I suspect that Jan might have already arrived

If there is no past participle, the order is either modal + infinitive or infinitive + modal:

   *Hij zegt dat dat het geval **kan** zijn/zijn **kan***
   He says that that might be the case

II   *kunnen* is not always used as a modal auxiliary:

   Hij kan zwemmen
   He can swim

This is a statement of fact and does not convey the speaker's attitude. This different use of *kunnen* is reflected in the translation which uses a different verb in English: 'can' as opposed to 'might'. Another difference is that *kunnen,* **when not used modally, can occur in the perfect tense:**

> *Hij heeft vanaf zijn vijfde kunnen zwemmen*
> He has been able to swim since he was five

The verbal construction consists of perfect auxiliary *heeft* in 2nd place + (*kunnen* + infinitive) at the end of the sentence. These last two elements cannot be split up. This is an unusual construction because the perfect tense is constructed without a past participle. This has been replaced by the infinitive *kunnen*:

> *Ik weet dat hij vanaf zijn vijfde heeft kunnen zwemmen*
> I know that he has been able to swim since he was five

The word order for this construction in a subclause is: perfect auxiliary *hebben* + *kunnen* + infinitive.

III   *kunnen* can be used independently, i.e. without an infinitive, in certain fixed expressions:

> *Dat kan*   That is possible
> *Dat kan geen kwaad*   That can't do any harm
> *Het had beter gekund*   It could have been done better

This is the only time the past participle of *kunnen* is used.

MOETEN

I   *moeten* expresses probability when used modally and can only occur in the present and past tenses in this function:

> *Je moet vreselijk moe zijn*
> You must be terribly tired

Here, the modal is in 2nd place + the infinitive in final position.

The other verb can occur in the perfect:

> *Ze moeten zich die avond verveeld hebben*
> They must have been bored that evening

This shows the modal in 2nd place + (past participle + infinitive perfect auxiliary).

The sentences below illustrate the position of the verbal elements in a subclause. They are grouped together at the end of the clause in the following order: (past participle +) modal + infinitive.

Ik denk dat die mensen de nieuwe buren moeten zijn
I think that those people must be the new neighbours

Ik geloof dat hij heel ambitieus geweest moet zijn
I think that he must have been very ambitious

II   *moeten* is not always used modally. In this case it conveys obligation or necessity. For example:

U moet zich haasten
You must hurry

The word order is still modal in 2nd place + infinitive in final position, but the translations 'ought/should/have to' are now also possible.

When it is not used modally, *moeten* can occur in the perfect tense:

Ze hebben terstond moeten vertrekken
They had to leave immediately

The perfect auxiliary *hebben* is in 2nd place with the infinitive of *moeten* + other infinitive in final place. Note that as with *kunnen,* the past participle has been replaced by the infinitive.

The order of elements in a subclause is (perfect auxiliary +) *moeten* + infinitive:

Ik vind dat je wel moet gaan
I think that you should/ought to go

Heb ik je verteld dat ik naar huis heb moeten gaan?
Did I tell you that I had to go home?

III   *moeten* can be used independently, i.e. without an infinitive, in certain expressions:

Het moest
It had to be done

Het heeft zo gemoeten
It had to be (done) like that

This is the only time the past participle is used.

IV   When the negative of *moeten* is required to convey that there is no obligation, *hoeven* replaces *moeten,* as in

Je moet het doen
You must do it

but

Je hoeft het niet te doen
You don't have to do it

When *hoeven* is used, the infinitive is preceded by *te.*

MOGEN

I   When used modally, *mogen* conveys that the speaker is conceding something. *Mogen* is only used in the present and past tenses in this function. For example:

Hij mag wel rijk zijn, aardig is hij niet
He may be rich but he isn't nice (to know)

In this function, *mogen* itself cannot occur in the perfect, but the other verb can:

Zij mag dan veel gelezen hebben, veel weet ze niet
She may have read a lot but she doesn't know much

There is a special construction using the past tense *mocht(en)* at the beginning of a sentence to express 'if ...':

Mocht u iets nodig hebben, dan kunt u het bij mij lenen
If you should need anything, you can borrow it from me

In English it is also possible to start with the verb: 'should you need anything …'

II   When not used modally, *mogen* expresses the freedom to do something, translating English 'may/be allowed':

Je mag hier roken
You may smoke here

Mogen can occur in the perfect tense in this meaning:

Dat hebben wij als kinderen nooit mogen doen
We were never allowed to do that as children

In this case the perfect auxiliary *hebben* is in 2nd place and *mogen* + infinitive are in final position.

The order in a subclause is: *hebben* + *mogen* + infinitive, all in final position. For example:

Mijn broer zegt dat wij dat nooit hebben mogen doen
My brother says that we were never allowed to do that

Sometimes *mogen* also translates English 'ought/should':

He **ought** to be pleased he was allowed to stay
*Hij **mag** wel blij zijn dat hij mocht blijven*

III   *mogen* can be used independently:

Dat mag
That is allowed

Hij mag vandaag niet uit
He is not allowed out today

WILLEN

I   The modal use of *willen* is not such an important function of this verb. It is used to imply that what is described in the rest of the sentence happens sometimes. *Willen* can only occur in the present and past tenses in this function. For example:

Geef hem een aspirientje, dat wil wel eens helpen
Give him an aspirin, that sometimes helps

There is also a construction with *willen* in first place which expresses 'if …':

Hij moet veel oefenen, wil hij de wedstrijd winnen
He must practise a lot if he is to win the match

II   The most frequent use of *willen* is as a non-modal verb meaning 'want/wish':

Ik wil hier altijd blijven
I want to stay here for ever

In this, *willen* is in 2nd place + infinitive in final position.

In this function, *willen* can occur in the perfect. The past participle is replaced by the infinitive *willen*:

Zij heeft die film altijd willen zien
She has always wanted to see that film

This construction has the perfect auxiliary *hebben* in 2nd place + (*willen* + infinitive) which occur together in final position.

The subclause word order is (*hebben* +) *willen* + infinitive all in final position:

Ze zegt dat ze dat boek altijd heeft willen lezen
She says that she has always wanted to read that book

III   *willen* can also be used independently without an infinitive:

Hij wil wel
He wants to

Dat heeft zij altijd gewild
She has always wanted that

ZULLEN

I   When used modally, *zullen* expresses probability. It is only found in the present and past tense in this use:

Hij zal wel slagen
He will probably pass (the exam)

The other verb (e.g. *slagen*) can occur in the perfect:

Hij zal wel geslaagd zijn
He will probably have passed

II   **The past tense of *zullen* + infinitive is used to form the conditional of Dutch verbs.** This corresponds to English 'would' + infinitive.

Model conjugation of conditional of *gaan*:

ik zou gaan	I would go
jij zou gaan	you would go
u zou gaan	you would go
hij zou gaan	he would go
wij zouden gaan	we would go
jullie zouden gaan	you would go
u zou gaan	you would go
zij zouden gaan	they would go

The use of the conditional in Dutch is the same as in English except that some Dutch conditionals are rendered by the imperfect in English:

Als ik dat zou doen ....
If I did that ....

III   *zullen* is the auxiliary verb used to form the future tense (see p.22). However, this tense in Dutch is more emphatic than in English and is also used less frequently than in English. The sentence

> *Ik zal het doen*
> I will do it

implies some sort of commitment on the part of the speaker.

IV   The past tense of *zullen* is used in polite requests, usually with another of the verbs in this group:

> *Zou u kunnen komen?*
> Would you be able to come?
> *Zou je dit voor me willen doen?*
> Would you do this for me?

V   *zullen* is also used independently:

> *Dat zal wel*
> *lit.* That will probably = I expect so

2) *blijken, lijken, schijnen*

These verbs convey the speaker's attitude to whether something is a fact; *lijken* and *schijnen* express the speaker's uncertainty...

> *Hij lijkt/schijnt wel intelligent te zijn*
> He seems to be intelligent

whereas *blijken* indicates that the speaker has ascertained something:

> *Hij blijkt intelligent te zijn*
> He is shown/turns out to be intelligent

Unlike the verbs in group 1, these verbs are always modal and — like group 1 verbs when used modally — can *only* be used in the present and past tenses. The modal verb is in 2nd place in the sentence with *te* + infinitive in final position.

When the modal verb is used with a separable verb, *te* comes between prefix and basic verb:

Zij schijnt op te letten
She seems to pay attention

Although the modal itself cannot occur in the perfect tenses, the other verb can. For example:

Hij blijkt hard gewerkt te hebben
He turns out to have worked hard

Zij schijnt opgelet te hebben
She seems to have paid attention

In a subclause, the modal forms a group with the other verbal elements in final position:

Ik hoor dat de nieuwe buurman vriendelijk schijnt te zijn
I hear that the new neighbour seems to be friendly

The order of verbal elements is: modal + *te* + infinitive.

Positional verbs - *hangen, liggen, lopen, staan, zitten*

These verbs are used to specify the position of the subject while performing the action denoted by another verb. They are most frequently translated by 'to be' in English.

De was hangt te drogen
The washing is drying

Zij ligt te slapen
She is sleeping

Het kind liep te zeuren
The child was whining

Zij staan te praten
They are talking

Hij zit een boek te lezen
He is reading a book

The positional verb is in second place and the infinitive preceded by *te* is in final position.

In the perfect tenses, the past participle of the positional verb is replaced by the infinitive:

Hij heeft een boek zitten (te) lezen
He has been reading a book

The perfect auxiliary *hebben* is now in second place and the verb phrase in final position consists of: positional infinitive + *(te +)* infinitive.

In a subclause, all the verbs form a group in final position consisting of the following:

present & past tense: positional + *te* + infinitive
perfect tenses: *hebben* + positional infinitive + *(te +)* infinitive

Mijn zus zegt dat de jongen liep te huilen
My sister says that the boy was crying

Ik hoor dat ze de hele dag hebben zitten (te) werken
I hear that they have been working the whole day long

Other verbs which form compound verbal constructions

These verbs fall into two groups according to the way their compound verbal constructions are formed.

1) These verbs are used with an infinitive, and in the perfect tenses the past participle of the verb is replaced by its infinitive, i.e. they behave like group 1 modal verbs. They are listed below:

INFINITIVE	EXAMPLE
blijven	*Zij bleef werken*
to continue	She continued working
doen	*Dat deed me schrikken*
to make	That made me jump
gaan	*Wij gaan winkelen*
to go	We are going shopping
helpen	*Ik heb hem helpen ontsnappen*
to help	I helped him escape
horen	*Ik hoorde jou zingen*
to hear	I heard you singing
komen	*Zij komt de auto terugbrengen*
to come	She's coming to bring the car back
laten	*Hij heeft zijn haar laten knippen*
to have	He has had his hair cut
leren	*Ik leerde haar zwemmen*
to teach	I taught her to swim
ruiken	*Ik ruik iets branden*
to smell	I (can) smell something burning
vinden	*Ze vonden hem op de grond liggen*
to find	They found him lying on the ground
voelen	*Ik voel het regenen*
to feel	I (can) feel it raining
zien	*Ik heb jullie in het café zien zitten*
to see	I saw you sitting in the café

2) This group of verbs is used with an infinitive preceded by *te*. The list below gives the main verbs in this category. They do not all form their perfect tenses in the same way, so this will be indicated with each verb.

INFINITIVE	PERF. TENSE WITH	EXAMPLE
beginnen	past part.	*Ik was begonnen te spelen*
to begin		I had started to play

beloven	past part.	*Hij heeft beloofd te komen*
to promise		He has promised to come
besluiten	past part.	*Hij heeft besloten te komen*
to decide		He has decided to come
dreigen	past part.	*Hij heeft gedreigd weg te gaan*
to threaten		He threatened to leave
durven	infin.	*Ik heb niet durven (te) kijken*
to dare		I have not dared to look
eisen	past part.	*Ik heb geëist hem te zien*
to demand		I have demanded to see him
hopen	past part.	*Ik had gehoopt te komen*
to hope		I had hoped to come
(be)horen	infin.	*Hij heeft horen te betalen*
ought		He ought to have paid
krijgen	—	*Ik kreeg haar vandaag te zien*
to get		I got to see her today
menen	past part.	*Hij heeft gemeend te kunnen komen*
to think		
		He thought he could come
proberen	past part.	*Wij hebben geprobeerd te spreken*
to try		We have tried to speak
trachten	past part.	*Ik heb getracht mijn best te doen*
to try		I have tried to do my best
vallen	—	*Het valt niet te betwisten*
be able		It can't be disputed
verbieden	past part.	*Ik heb hem verboden te gaan*
to forbid		I have forbidden him to go
vergeten	past part.	*Hij heeft vergeten op te bellen*
to forget		He has forgotten to ring up
verklaren	past part.	*Zij heeft verklaard te zullen spelen*
to declare		She has declared she will play
verlangen	past part.	*Ze hebben verlangd elkaar te zien*
to long		They have longed to see one another
vragen	past part.	*Hij heeft gevraagd te gaan*
to ask		He has asked to go

vrezen	past part.	*Ik heb gevreesd haar te zien*
to fear		I was afraid of seeing her
wagen	past part.	*Heb je gewaagd het te doen?*
to dare		Have you dared to do it?
weigeren	past part.	*Hij heeft geweigerd het te doen*
to refuse		He refused to do it
wensen	past part.	*Ik heb gewenst haar te zien*
to wish		I wished to see her
weten	infin.	*Hij heeft weten te ontsnappen*
to manage		He managed to escape
zeggen	past part.	*Ze hebben gezegd geld te hebben*
to say		They said they had money

Use of tenses in Dutch

Although we use the same labels such as *present* and *perfect* for tenses in both Dutch and English, the way these tenses are used differs. So in addition to learning how to form the tenses of Dutch verbs, it is also necessary to learn how to use them in order to speak and write correct Dutch.

One major difference between the two languages is that English has twice as many tenses as Dutch, because each tense in English also has a continuous form:

I write   =   simple present
I am writing   =   continuous present

In general, Dutch renders the English continuous tenses by other means than tense. These are given in detail on pp.82-83.

Present tense

The present tense is more widely used in Dutch than in English. It refers both to the present and to the future. For example:

Ik schrijf een brief   =   present time
I am writing a letter

Morgen schrijf ik hem   =   future time
I'll write to him tomorrow

Note that an English continuous tense can also be rendered by the Dutch present tense. This means that there are two possible translations of a present tense in Dutch:

Hij zingt   He sings AND He is singing

As in English, the present tense is used to indicate a repeated action:

Ik kom hier elke dag
I come here every day

However, it is also used in Dutch to indicate a state of affairs which continues up to the present, whereas English uses a perfect.

Ik werk hier al zes jaar
I have been working here for six years

Past tense

The past tense in Dutch is less widely used than the past tense in English. This is because the English past tense is frequently rendered by a present perfect in Dutch:

Then we bought a new car	simple past
Toen hebben wij een nieuwe auto gekocht	pres. perfect

The translation

Toen kochten wij een nieuwe auto	simple past

is also possible, but less usual, particularly in spoken Dutch where a perfect sounds more natural.

The past tense is used more frequently with the verbs *hebben* and *zijn*. For example:

Hoe was de lezing?
How was the lecture?

Ik had mijn fototoestel bij me
I had my camera with me

The past tense is always used after the conjunction *toen* (when).

Toen hij me zag, liep hij meteen weg
When he saw me, he immediately ran off

The past tense in Dutch can have a modal function, i.e. it can serve to express the speaker's attitude. When used this way, it is actually a contraction of a conditional. Compare

Hij moest eten   past tense
He had to eat

which is a statement of fact, with

Jij moest meer eten   contracted conditional
(Jij zou meer moeten eten)
i.e.
You should eat more

which clearly conveys the speaker's attitude to the necessity of the action denoted by the verb. The past tense can be used in this way with the following verbs:

INFINITIVE	PAST	TRANSLATION	MODAL	TRANSLATION
moeten	*moest*	had to	*moest*	should
kunnen	*kon*	was able/could	*kon*	could
mogen	*mocht*	was allowed	*mocht*	should
willen	*wou*	wanted	*wou*	would (like)

Dutch has other ways of rendering the English continuous past. See pp.82-83.

Future tense

The future tense refers to future time in both English and Dutch. However, it is less widely used in Dutch because the present is also used to refer to future time. The future tense in Dutch is more emphatic. Compare

Ik zal het morgen doen   with *Ik doe het morgen*
I *will* do it tomorrow   I'll do it tomorrow

Present perfect

This tense is used very differently in Dutch, although **all English present perfects are rendered by the present perfect in Dutch.** In addition to this, **most English simple past tenses can be rendered in Dutch by the present perfect,** and this is more likely to be so in the spoken language.

I have seen him	present perfect
Ik heb hem gezien	present perfect
Then I saw him	simple past
Toen heb ik hem gezien	present perfect

Past & future perfect

The use of these tenses corresponds to their use in English.

How to deal with English continuous tenses

The continuous tenses in English are formed with the verb 'to be' + -ing.

he is eating	present
he was eating	past
he will be eating	future
he has been eating	present perfect
he had been eating	past perfect
he will have been eating	future perfect

So where Dutch has one present tense, English has two, and this applies to all six tenses. One way of translating an English continuous tense is to ignore the continuous aspect and use a simple tense in Dutch.

She is writing a book	present cont.
Zij schrijft een boek	present
We were sitting in the garden	past cont.
Wij zaten in de tuin	past
We will be coming	future cont.
Wij zullen komen	future
You have been working hard	pres. perf. cont.
U hebt hard gewerkt	pres. perf.
I had been working too hard	past perf. cont.
Ik had te hard gewerkt	past perf.
She will have been living here for six years	future perf. cont.
Zij zal hier zes jaar gewoond hebben	future perf.

When the emphasis is on the action being performed, Dutch uses other constructions. This makes it possible to distinguish between 'they drink wine' *(zij drinken wijn)* and 'they are drinking wine'; in Dutch, the latter can be rendered as (i) *zij zijn wijn aan het drinken,* or (ii) *zij zitten wijn te drinken.* These two constructions are explained below:

i) *zijn* + *aan het* + **infinitive**
Zijn is the finite verb in 2nd place in the sentence, and the phrase *aan het* (usually contracted to *aan 't*) + infinitive is in final position. This construction can be used in all tenses.

Ik ben aan 't schrijven
I am writing

Ik was aan 't schrijven
I was writing

Ik zal morgen weer aan 't schrijven zijn
I shall be writing again tomorrow

Ik ben aan 't schrijven geweest
I have been writing etc.

Note that any other verbal elements which are placed at the end of the sentence always come after *aan 't* + infinitive. This also applies in subclauses.

Ik hoorde dat ze aan 't schilderen zijn geweest
I heard that they had been painting

ii) **positional verb** + *te* + **infinitive**
The positional verbs are: *hangen, liggen, lopen, staan, zitten.*

Zij zitten naar de tv te kijken
They are (sitting) watching TV

Note that the positional can sometimes be translated into English, giving a double -ing construction, as in 'sitting watching'. When translating English 'to be' into Dutch, it is important to choose the correct positional verb. For example, 'they are drinking wine' could be translated as *zij zitten wijn te drinken,* or *zij staan wijn te drinken,* or even *zij liggen wijn te drinken,* depending on their position at the time!
For the formation of the perfect tenses of this construction, see p.74.

How to deal with English 'put' and 'be'

One difference between Dutch and English verbs is that the Dutch language is much more specific when rendering English 'put' and 'be'. Dutch has three verbs for each: *zetten, leggen, stoppen* (put) and *staan, liggen, zitten* (be).

zetten is used when objects are placed in an upright position:

> *Zet het boek in de boekenkast*
> Put the book in the bookcase

The corresponding translation of 'to be' is *staan*:

> *Het boek staat in de boekenkast*
> The book is in the bookcase

leggen is used when objects are placed so that they lie flat on a surface:

> *Leg het boek op tafel*
> Put the book on the table

The corresponding translation of 'to be' is *liggen*:

> *Het boek ligt op tafel*
> The book is on the table

stoppen is used when an object is placed inside something:

> *Stop het boek in mijn tas*
> Put the book in my bag

The corresponding translation of 'to be' is *zitten*:

> *Het boek zit in mijn tas*
> The book is in my bag

Verbs used with a fixed preposition

Many Dutch verbs have a **preposition object.** This means that the object of the verb is preceded by a preposition. The verbs in this group are always used with the same preposition, which we describe as fixed because the speaker has no choice in the selection of the preposition.

In the sentence *Ik wacht op mijn zus* ('I am waiting for my sister'), *op* is the fixed preposition and *mijn zus* is the preposition object. It is not possible simply to translate the preposition from English into Dutch, because it often has a special meaning in these constructions. *Op* usually renders English 'on', for instance, but is translated here as 'for', and *geloven **aan*** is translated as 'believe **in**', even though *aan* usually renders 'at/to'. In other words, **these prepositions cannot be guessed at: they have to be learned.** The main Dutch verbs with a fixed preposition will be listed below in 13 groups according to which preposition they use.

Since the lists are extensive, including verbs which form part of phrases like *behoefte hebben aan* (to need), they will also serve as vocabulary lists for broadening your repertoire of verbs.

GROUP 1 — VERBS WHICH USE *aan*

zich aanpassen aan	to adapt to
behoefte hebben aan	to need
beantwoorden aan	to correspond to
behoren aan	to belong to
bijdragen aan	to contribute to
deelnemen aan	to take part in
denken aan	to think of
zich ergeren aan	to be irritated by
geloven aan	to believe in
grenzen aan	to border on
herinneren aan	to remind of
zich houden aan	to keep to

lenen aan	to lend to
lijden aan	to suffer from
meedoen aan	to join in with
onderwerpen aan	to subject to
ontgroeien aan	to grow out of
ontkomen aan	to evade
ontsnappen aan	to escape from
overlijden aan	to die from
sterven aan	to die from
toeschrijven aan	to attribute to
toevertrouwen aan	to entrust to
toevoegen aan	to add to
twijfelen aan	to doubt
voldoen aan	to comply with
voorafgaan aan	to precede
wanhopen aan	to despair of
wennen aan	to get used to
werken aan	to work on
zich wijden aan	to devote oneself to

GROUP 2 — VERBS WHICH USE *bij*

belang hebben bij	to have an interest in
betrokken zijn bij	to be involved in
behoren bij	to belong with
zich neerleggen bij	to go along with
passen bij	to match
vergelijken bij	to compare with
zweren bij	to swear by

GROUP 3 — VERBS WHICH USE *in*

aankomen in	to arrive in
berusten in	to resign oneself to
gelijk hebben in	to be right about
geloven in	to believe in
slagen in	to succeed at/in

zich specialiseren in	to specialize in
trek/zin hebben in	to feel like
veranderen in	to change into
zich verdiepen in	to be engrossed in
volharden in	to persist in
voorzien in	to supply

GROUP 4 — VERBS WHICH USE *met*

zich bemoeien met	to interfere in
zich bezighouden met	to be occupied in/with
dwepen met	to be mad about
feliciteren met	to congratulate on
gelijkstaan met	to be on a par with
overeenkomen met	to correspond to/with
overeenstemmen met	to be in agreement with
spotten met	to mock
trouwen met	to marry
verbinden met	to link to
verenigen met	to unite with
vergelijken met	to compare with
volstaan met	to make do with
het eens zijn met	to agree with

GROUP 5 — VERBS WHICH USE *naar*

begerig zijn naar	to desire
benieuwd zijn naar	to be curious about
dorsten naar	to thirst after
geuren naar	to smell of
gissen naar	to guess at
hunkeren naar	to hanker after
informeren naar	to inquire about
kijken naar	to watch/look at
luisteren naar	to listen to
nieuwsgierig zijn naar	to be curious about
oordelen naar	to judge from

ruiken naar	to smell of
smaken naar	to taste of
solliciteren naar	to apply for
staren naar	to stare at
streven naar	to strive for
uitkijken naar	to look out for
uitzien naar	to look out for
verlangen naar	to long for
verwijzen naar	to refer to
vragen naar	to ask for
wijzen naar	to point to
zoeken naar	to look for

GROUP 6 — VERBS WHICH USE *om*

bedelen om	to beg for
zich bekommeren om	to worry about
bidden om	to pray for
denken om	to think about/remember
geven om	to care about
huilen om	to cry about
lachen om	to laugh about
smeken om	to plead for
treuren om	to grieve for
verzoeken om	to request
vragen om	to ask for
wedden om	to bet on
wenen om	to weep for

GROUP 7 — VERBS WHICH USE *op*

aandringen op	to insist on
zich abonneren op	to subscribe to
acht geven op	to pay attention to
antwoorden op	to answer to
bedacht zijn op	to be intent on
zich beroepen op	to appeal to

berusten op	to be based on
betrekking hebben op	to relate to
drinken op	to drink to
duiden op	to point to
hopen op	to hope for
ingaan op	to go into (a matter)
jagen op	to hunt
kijken op	to look at (a watch)
kritiek hebben op	to be critical of
lijken op	to resemble
letten op	to pay attention to
mikken op	to aim at
neerkomen op	to come down to
passen op	to look after
reageren op	to react to
rekenen op	to count on
richten op	to direct at
schatten op	to value at
schelden op	to scold
schieten op	to shoot at
staan op	to insist on
steunen op	to rest on
storten op	to pay into
terugkomen op	to come back to
zich toeleggen op	to apply oneself to
toepassen op	to apply to
trakteren op	to treat to
uitlopen op	to result in
zich verheugen op	to look forward to
vertrouwen op	to depend on
vloeken op	to curse
volgen op	to follow after/on
voorbereiden op	to prepare for
vuren op	to fire on
wachten op	to wait for
wijzen op	to point out/to
zinspelen op	to allude to

GROUP 8 — VERBS WHICH USE *over*

zich beklagen over	to lament
beschikken over	to have at one's disposal
beslissen over	to decide about
denken over	to think about
zich druk maken over	to make a fuss about
het eens zijn over	to agree about
zich ergeren over	to get upset about
heersen over	to rule over
huilen over	to cry about
jammeren over	to wail about
klagen over	to complain about
oordelen over	to judge
peinzen over	to ponder (on)
praten over	to talk about
regeren over	to govern
roddelen over	to gossip about
zich schamen over	to be ashamed about
schrijven over	to write about
spreken over	to speak about
tobben over	to worry about
zich uitspreken over	to pronounce about
zich verbazen over	to be amazed at
zich verheugen over	to rejoice at
vertellen over	to tell about
waken over	to watch over
wenen over	to weep over
zaniken over	to moan about
zegevieren over	to triumph over
zeuren over	to whine about

GROUP 9 — VERBS WHICH USE *tegen*

beschermen tegen	to protect against
glimlachen tegen	to smile at
kampen tegen	to fight against

knikken tegen	to nod at
opzien tegen	to dread; to look up at
ruilen tegen	to exchange for
spreken tegen	to speak to
uitvaren tegen	to lash out at
zich verzetten tegen	to resist
wisselen tegen	to change for
zeggen tegen	to say to

GROUP 10 — VERBS WHICH USE *tot*

aansporen tot	to incite to
aanzetten tot	to incite to
behoren tot	to belong to
zich berperken tot	to limit oneself to
bereid zijn tot	to be ready for
bidden tot	to pray to
bijdragen tot	to contribute to
dienen tot	to serve as
kiezen tot	to elect/choose as
noodzaken tot	to necessitate
zich richten tot	to turn/apply to
spreken tot	to speak to
strekken tot	to serve as
veroordelen tot	to condemn to
zich wenden tot	to turn to

GROUP 11 — VERBS WHICH USE *uit*

afleiden uit	to deduce from
bestaan uit	to consist of
drinken uit	to drink from
komen uit	to come from
groeien uit	to grow out of
ontstaan uit	to spring/arise from
opmaken uit	to conclude from

verbannen uit	to banish from
vertalen uit	to translate from
vervaardigen uit	to manufacture from
voortvloeien uit	to result from

GROUP 12 — VERBS WHICH USE *van*

afhangen van	to depend on
afstammen van	to be descended from
afzien van	to give up
balen van	to be fed up with
zich bedienen van	to make use of
beroven van	to deprive of
beschuldigen van	to accuse of
bevrijden van	to free from
dromen van	to dream of
genieten van	to enjoy
houden van	to like/love
krioelen van	to teem with
leven van	to live on
zich onthouden van	to abstain from
overtuigen van	to convince of
scheiden van	to separate from
schrikken van	to be frightened by
veranderen van	to change
verdenken van	to suspect of
verschillen van	to differ from
voorzien van	to supply with
walgen van	to be disgusted by
wemelen van	to teem with/be full of
weten van	to know of/about

GROUP 13 — VERBS WHICH USE *voor*

bang zijn voor	to be afraid of
bezwijken voor	to yield to
danken voor	to thank for

zich hoeden voor	to beware of
zich interesseren voor	to be interested in
oppassen voor	to look out for
slagen voor	to pass
terugdeinzen voor	to shrink from
zich uitgeven voor	to pass for
vrezen voor	to fear for
waarschuwen voor	to warn against
zakken voor	to fail
zorgen voor	to look after/take care of